Create
Your Day
With Intention!

The

30-Day

Power Coach

Vicki H. Escudé, M.A., MCC
Master Certified Coach

Escudé, Vicki H.
        Create Your Day With Intention! The 30-Day Power
Coach

ISBN 0-9705307-1-4

        1. Personal development. 2. Attraction Theory.
        3. Coaching. 4. Self-Help. 5. Goal Setting. 6. Success.
        7. Career development

**Attention: For copies and information, contact Vicki
Escudé, Executive Leadership Coaching, LLC, at
Vicki@excellentcoach.com, or www.excellentcoach.com.
Discounts available for quantities.**

Books by Vicki Escudé

*Getting Everything You Want and Going for More!
Coaching for Mastery*

A Year on the Yard

*150 Yesteryears: Families, Homes and Treasured
Memories of the USNA*

Gifts of the Spirit

*Create Your Day with Intention! The 30-Day Power
Coach*

This book is dedicated to the Bright Spirits of Leon, Laura and Chandler!

About Vicki Escudé as a Success Coach, and Coach Trainer:

How grateful I am that you have been in my life with your powerful presence and training. Thank you for being a part of the fabric of my life! Love, light and hugs! *Kim Yancey, Successful Life Coaching*

Vicki, you are an excellent coach with such a broad range of skills. You are always competent no matter the subject or issue. This has been a life altering experience and I am grateful. *Wanda Taylor, MCC, Bay Centre Counseling*

To a terrific coach! Thanks so much for being a part of my life of new beginnings. To clarify my calling has been my passion. You have been a mirror in so many ways and have shone a light on my path. *C. A.*

The program taught me focus and accountability. I also became better organized and learned to set priorities. *J.V.*

I was quite pleased with the overall program. Vicki did a great job – she is understanding and easily finds learning experiences in negative situations. Vicki helps you focus on the future. She teaches you that today's challenges are the building blocks for tomorrow's successes. I am pleased with my coaching experience and have implemented many facets into my life. *K. L.*

Contents

Forward

Create your own *magic,* allow inner gifts and outer shifts, and notice the clues that will build your trust in the perfect unfolding of a new YOU! Begin attracting what you want in life!

Achieving goals and creating a new life involve increasing your inner awareness and changing old patterns. The ability to change patterns is enhanced by being open to fresh ideas, and fresh ideas nurture a new awareness of who you are and who you choose to be.

This little book can be your feast for new ideas, your personal coach for personal and professional transformation. You will find tools for self-reflection, tools for action, and tools for personal growth.

<u>Create Your Day With Intention! The 30-Day Power Coach</u> will invite your genius out to play, so that you can build on your dreams. Daily you will learn powerful tools to help you experience the joy of intentional living using the magic wand of gratitude.

This book will help you heighten your self-awareness, clarify your intentions and maintain your focus. In 30 days, you can transform who you are, acknowledge your inner strengths, and create a more satisfying, fulfilling life.

A playful attitude is essential. Enjoying your participation raises your vibrations and attracts what you want to you. The topics are designed to support a positive energy shift. The most important thing you can bring to this playground is your enjoyment of the process.

In 30 days you can design a life you choose. You have your own brilliant, resident genius within you, an inner architect for your designer life.

Let this be your playground. Begin now!

Introduction

By
Teri-E Belf, M.A., C.A.G.S., M.C.C.

Are you ready for a powerful uplifting experience *right now*? Stop reading my words and skip to the Table of Contents... Sounds like a formula for success? Just a sneak preview.

If you are one of the hundreds of people who has had the good fortune to have met or worked with Vicki then you have probably thought, "How can I put her on the copy machine and take her with me?" We have those thoughts when we are in the presence of someone who talks and acts congruently, and seems to consistently gain clarity about what is desired, focuses action to that end, and succeeds. Well Vicki has copied and collated herself into this little book and you can take 'her' with you.

In the opening sentence of the Forward Escudé uses the word magic. Playing with this book feels like magic. Magic... when we do not understand how something happens and yet we see or hear it happen. You have seen magic tricks. You know there is a secret how to do them, yet you don't know the secret. I have two expert magicians in my family, members of high regard in the magical society. I know they understand how to do their tricks because they study and practice until they can create the illusion. They won't tell me how because there is an ethical code in their profession. Magic happens without me knowing how. Manifestation, although appearing magical at times, is different. We can learn how.

11

It's all in this tiny book.

Now come the buts.

"Only 30 days", you say, "That's hard to believe. I've been trying to get what I want for years. How is this book any different from all the other books on my shelf?"

Truthfully, it isn't. The magic is that YOU are holding THIS book NOW. And maybe, just maybe, THIS IS THE TIME you are ready, really ready to attract what you want.

Next argument. "But it takes time and I don't even have enough time now to do everything." Gotcha! That is one of the reasons for this book. If you could purchase the ability, the potential, the wisdom to have enough time to get what you want, would you buy it? If you say no, put this book down. Otherwise, buy it and begin.

"But," you challenge me, "it does take time." It took me 24 seconds to read one of the Daily Success Tips. Just 24 seconds. In business lingo we ask what is the opportunity cost or, what did I have to give up to choose this instead? No way you could convince me that you had a more meaningful and useful 24 seconds prioritized game plan for each of the next 30 days. A blip in the number of moments in your human lifetime. Just 24 seconds. A more powerful question is what are you giving up by *not* using these 24 seconds to be intentional?

Let's say you cannot find 24 seconds, you might consider reading the daily Affirmation at the bottom of each Daily Success Tip. That takes about 2 seconds, ok, maybe 4 if you linger.

"But this requires a huge commitment to myself," you protest. If you won't commit to yourself, who will?

One of Escudé's key principles is that attraction is about your inner work first. Think about this, when you look in a mirror and see messy hair, you don't comb the mirror. You still need to pick up the comb and use it! To participate with manifestation, pick up this book and declare your first intention: to use it.

Caution: this book will actually disappear if you put it on your bookshelf. Trust your bookshelf to be responsible for doing its own inner work. Place this book right by your bedside so you can begin and end your day with your inner work.

"Yes, but it sounds too good to be true", you are thinking. What's wrong with good being true?

Your excuse tank is empty.

Escudé's philosophy is that your day is like a gift. You unwrap it in the morning, unleash its uniqueness and specialness throughout the day, and then, with a heart-felt thank you, wrap it up at night. What feels magical is that every day is a different gift. You get to choose the color and texture of the wrapping paper, the color and design of the bows and ribbons, the shape of the gift box and even what is inside. You get to choose. What fun!

That is an important theme throughout the book, be playful. Admittedly most of us like to look at the wrapping paper, ribbons and bows; however, we like even better opening the gift and discovering what is inside.

Escudé has let the secret out. With this book you can become your own manifestation magician. How to manifest is not a secret when you use the right tool and have the right guide to assist you. This book is your tool and Escudé is your guide. Through living language (the book practically breathes on its own), Escudé offers easy-to-do and thought-provoking exercises documented to learn and practice attraction. *Create Your Day With Intention* provides you with the structure and techniques through Daily Success Tips, affirmations, even the daily page to journal your morning intentions and evening gratitude notes.

I am lucky to be Vicki's colleague and have attended many of her training presentations about intention, attraction and manifestation. She lives what she is talking and writing about and she is passionate about sharing these techniques through her roles as coach, coach trainer and coaching leader, workshop presenter and author.

If you want to be inspired with some incredible manifestation stories, ask her, or, even better yet, tell her about your successes as you surf on a wave of your positive potential and engage in the magical playground of intentions using *Create Your Day With Intention.*

P.S. Each one of us is our personal magician. If you are holding this book, your magic is already happening.

Teri-E Belf is the Director and Founder of Success Unlimited Network®, LLC, an ICF accredited Coach

Training Program. She is the author of <u>Coaching with Spirit</u> and co-Author of <u>Simply Live it Up</u>, and <u>Auto Suggestions</u>.

How to play with this book:

❖ Place this book by your bedside with a pen or pencil.
❖ Smile.
❖ Read the short daily idea in the morning, and in the evening.
❖ Create a list of "Intentions" for the day each morning. Your intentions may or may not be related to the daily Success Tip.
❖ Continue to Smile.
❖ List thoughts of "gratitude" each evening.
❖ Release all negative patterns and worries before retiring.
❖ Smile once again.
❖ Continue this process for 30 days.
❖ You may go straight through the book or intuitively choose days at random.
❖ Review the book for the next 30 days.

This book is for:

■ Coaches
■ Mentors
■ Teachers
■ Students
■ Attractors
■ Truth Seekers
■ Coaching clients
■ People who want effortless change
■ People who want magic in their life!

How the tools in this book work:

Morning:

Morning time, before you get out of bed, is a time when your awakening self is open and fresh. Whatever you focus on at that time will influence and form your experiences for the day. Reading a new, inspiring idea and clearly focusing on how you truly want to BE that day using "Intentions," gives you a head start toward successful daily experiences.

Bedtime:

Bedtime is a time to unwind, reinforce new ideas, and reflect on positives for the day using the vehicle of "Gratitude." The inner self will begin to look for and attract positive experiences during your daytime so that you can notice them in the evening. Before you sleep, release any negative patterns and worry from the past and allow them to stop at that time, so that you will wake truly refreshed with a clean slate for your new day.

Here are some suggestions to assist you to release worry and negative emotions as you prepare to drift off into sleep:

1. As you breath in, think, "I allow healing within me." As you breathe out, think, "I release worry and other negative thoughts and feelings now."
2. Write down all the "to-do's" crowding your mind, and plan to move forward with them the next day.

3. Imagine putting all of your worries into a sack, and giving them to your Higher Self, your angels, or God to hold for you during the night.

Practicing positive self-talk and setting up positive expectations on a daily basis will help you develop new patterns for success. The individual tools within the daily ideas will help you to move powerfully forward to achieve goals that are meaningful and purposeful to you.

After 30 days, new, positive patterns are in place. A new you is born!

Part I

Clarify

~Clarify~

Life sometimes seems to happen "to" us. In **Part I** you will begin to experience the power of gratitude and the joy of setting your own intentions, loosening up your ability to dream. Your mind will gently move you toward creating a vision as well as meaningful goals. Access your inner genius, the architect for your new life, by getting in touch with what you REALLY want.

Day 1

Daily Success Tip:

Be Intentional

More energizing than morning coffee!
Do you want to enrich the quality of your life, but find yourself jumping out of bed each morning, grabbing that cup of coffee, rushing out, and having the same kind of day you always had?

Here is a simple idea to make a HUGE change in your life: write **Daily Intentions. Daily Intentions** are how you wish to experience your day – not a to-do list. It's easy!

> Step 1: Put this book and a pen or pencil beside your bed, and
> Step 2: Every morning write a short list of your intentions – how you want to **Be** for that day.

Example: I might write, "have fun being lighthearted today," and "keep a calm and steady focus on my goals," and "enjoy listening to my intuition today." These Intentions sound like "Affirmations," or positive statements about how you choose to BE today. Once you have written them, put them aside and let them go. Notice if you begin to experience your day differently.

That's it! Have fun using this new tool for focus and personal awareness.

> Affirmation: *I am intentional about how I choose to experience every day. I am amazed at how my success unfolds.*

Morning - Today I intend to experience:

    1.

    2.

    3.

    4.

    5.

Evening – Tonight I express gratitude for whatever made me happy today:

    1.

    2.

    3.

    4.

    5.

Day 2

Daily Success Tip:
Choose Gratitude

Tucked away on the bottom of a page in our local newspaper one week was a two-sentence article entitled: **"On the bright side: counting blessings is healthful."** Not as eye-catching as war or pestilence, so it didn't get top billing.

However, the article boldly states: *"New research shows that people who consciously remind themselves every day of the things they are grateful for show marked improvements in mental health and some aspects of physical health. The results appear to be equally true for healthy college students and people with incurable diseases, according to new research published in the Journal of Personality and Social Psychology."* *

There you have it!

Take Action: You may have heard about the power of a "Gratitude Journal." Here is a slightly different twist that, I've been told, produces great, significant changes in people's lives.

Every evening, before going to sleep, mentally identify or write down 5 things that happened that day that made you happy. It is fun!

Affirmation: *I recount my blessings daily, knowing that this is a powerful way to create the health and success I choose.*

---

*Savannah Morning News, News In Brief, wire reports 3/10/03

Morning - Today I intend to experience:

    1.

    2.

    3.

    4.

    5.

Evening – Tonight I express gratitude for whatever made me happy today:

    1.

    2.

    3.

    4.

    5.

Day 3

Daily Success Tip:
Create a Vision

Create a future **Vision**: Spend a few quiet moments either thinking about or visualizing how you would like your life to be different three months from now. Write your vision as a script, as if you are writing a scene in play in which you are the star! Make your vision "juicy" and compelling by adding "feeling" words. Use present-tense verbs, so that your vision-script sounds, looks and feels like you have already achieved what you want.

Ask yourself, "What new goals do I wish to create and what action steps will I take?" "How committed am I to this vision on a scale of 1 to 10?" "What would make this vision a '10' in commitment for me?" "How is this vision a reflection of my priorities and core values?"

Take Action: Write down your vision and your script and read it daily for 30 days. Enjoy the magic of attraction!

Affirmation: *I enjoy creating a clear and exciting vision of my life in the next three months. I attract success, and I am pleased!*

28

Morning - Today I intend to experience:

    1.

    2.

    3.

    4.

    5.

Evening – Tonight I express gratitude for whatever made me happy today:

    1.

    2.

    3.

    4.

    5.

Daily Success Tip:
Effortless Action

Do you know where your goals are?

We often groan when we hear the word, "goal." It sounds like a big, ugly, unwelcome, overwhelming "to-do list." We have often been taught to overwork and over-do goals. We think of multitudes of small steps that we take each day until the mountain has been climbed. We get tired.

Recent research tells us that most New Years Resolutions are forgotten or lost in the first few weeks of the year.

What works is to write down "dreams, intentions or results" you choose, picture them, say them, and then let go of making them happen. I like having them come to me "effortlessly," and then be surprised! I tell myself every morning, "Today I AM amazed at how my goals are unfolding." I let the universal wisdom and my Higher Self work their magic as I stay sharp for their cues to take action.

And, I express gratitude.

Affirmation: *Today I am amazed at how my goals are unfolding!*

Morning - Today I intend to experience:

    1.

    2.

    3.

    4.

    5.

Evening – Tonight I express gratitude for whatever made me happy today:

    1.

    2.

    3.

    4.

    5.

Day 5

Daily Success Tip:
Set Powerful Goals

Begin to consider your goals, your intentions and the results you choose. Take these powerful steps:

1. Choose one goal for each life area:

    > Appearance/Health
    > Career/Money
    > Fun/Leisure
    > Personal/Spiritual Development
    > Home-Work Environment
    > Relationships

2. Write these goals on 2 sheets of paper – one for your bedside, and one for your day-planner, PDA or wallet.

3. Read these goals at least 3 times per day – morning, noon, and night. Make them your best friends!

4. Partner with a coach or a friend for accountability.

Affirmation: *I choose who I become by being clear about my goals. I nurture these goals daily.*

Morning - Today I intend to experience:

    1.

    2.

    3.

    4.

    5.

Evening – Tonight I express gratitude for whatever made me happy today:

    1.

    2.

    3.

    4.

    5.

Day 6

Daily Success Tip:
The Twins: Dreams and Fears

There is an excitement and thrill that comes with new goals. However, hiding in the shadow of your Dream is its twin, Fear. In other words, expect resistance to loom large and have big hairy horns! Ah, my Friend, Fear! Welcome!

Most people do not get beyond the fear. They feel or think that something is wrong with their goal. They would much rather give up their goal than look at the fear. This resistance is natural, and an important function of the mind. Your mind's job is your "survival." It equates surviving with status quo, staying the same. "Stay the same," it whispers in your ear. "You won't survive if you try something new." Thank your mind for doing its job and helping you survive, and reassure it that you can change AND survive.

> *Spend some meditative or quiet time brainstorming possible stretches for yourself. A hint is to look at what you might have some fear around doing. The fear may be a clever cover-up for your passion or your next big step. Pick just one action or goal to "go for."*

Coaching can be a vital tool to use to get past the fear, and keep your focus on the goal.

Affirmation: *I am focused and continue moving toward my goals and visions.*

Morning - Today I intend to experience:

    1.

    2.

    3.

    4.

    5.

Evening – Tonight I express gratitude for whatever made me happy today:

    1.

    2.

    3.

    4.

    5.

Day 7

Daily Success Tip:
Take Small Steps

It is too late to begin on the road to success. (True or False?)

Often we think that we are too old, have a past that is too tainted, too unremarkable, or that it will take too much effort to "swim upstream" into success or positive change.

The past is merely your "school" in life. You can learn from all your experiences at any moment, and begin to set positive goals for yourself. Your success will be measured by your experience of the incredible and courageous journey you are taking.

Know that you can let go of the past and of past expectations. When you begin to break your big goals into tiny steps, and focus only on one at a time, the flow will begin, and at some point move you forward effortlessly. Often, it's the first tiny step that makes the difference.

Affirmation: *I begin today to choose a dream and goal, and take only one small step in that direction. I look for magical help along the way.*

Morning - Today I intend to experience:

    1.

    2.

    3.

    4.

    5.

Evening – Tonight I express gratitude for whatever made me happy today:

    1.

    2.

    3.

    4.

    5.

Day 8

Daily Success Tip:
Design a Dream

Being on automatic pilot daily diminishes our sense of aliveness. Take time to let loose of your old structures. Sit by the pool or on the beach, or pop some popcorn and watch an inspiring video - and allow yourself to dream about who you want to become, and where you want to go with your life.

Design a dream.

Tap into your passion by designing a dream. Move out of the "comfort zone," and into the "passing – or passion zone" by setting some stretch goals. When comfort sets in, begin to take some new risks and pump up your level of aliveness.

Take action: *Remember a time in your life when you were scared and you took action anyway? Recall the times you were thrilled by your outcomes.*

Have some FUN!

Affirmation: *I embrace new dreams, rekindle old dreams, and tap into my passion today. Stretching awakens my aliveness.*

Morning - Today I intend to experience:

    1.

    2.

    3.

    4.

    5.

Evening – Tonight I express gratitude for whatever made me happy today:

    1.

    2.

    3.

    4.

    5.

Powerful Questions for Part I

These questions will help deepen your learning and experiences with the "Create Your Day With Intention" process.

Read over your Intentions for Part I.

1. What do you notice?

   _____
   _____
   _____
   _____
   _____

2. Are you beginning to experience your days differently? If so, how?

   _____
   _____
   _____
   _____
   _____
   _____
   _____
   _____
   _____
   _____
   _____
   _____
   _____
   _____

_____

_____

Reflect on the visions and goals you developed in Part I.

   1. What are your thoughts and feelings about creating your visions and goals?

_____

_____

_____

_____

_____

_____

   2. Are you pleased with the goals you have chosen?

_____

_____

   3. Do your goals reflect who you want to become as a person? Describe that person.

_____

_____

_____

_____

   4. What obstacles do you fear?

_____

_____

_____

_____

_____

_____

_____

5. What are some possible solutions to those obstacles?

_____

_____

_____

_____

_____

_____

_____

_____

6. Who do you know that has achieved goals similar to yours, or who is like the person you choose to become?

_____

_____

_____

_____

7. What qualities do you have to support your visions and goals?

_____

_____

_____

_____

_____

_____

_____

_____

Part II

Simplify

~Simplify ~

Now that your visions and goals are clear, in **Part II** discover some underpinnings necessary for your grand design to unfold. Perhaps some old habits need to be recognized and replaced. Perhaps your goals need to become more real to you, and perhaps you can take some small steps toward activating and partnering with your inner genius.

Day 9

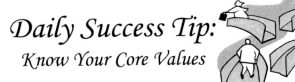

Daily Success Tip:
Know Your Core Values

Do you know your core values? Tapping into your core values and aligning your dreams with them, gives your goals more meaning. A value-based life is also a passionate, authentic life – just the juice you need to accomplish your goals!

Think of five people you admire. What are their top qualities? Are they things like endurance, fun, patience, enthusiasm, integrity, honesty, humility – or a myriad of other values?

The qualities you admire in them are also your core values, because what you see in others reflects what is meaningful to you.

So, take the top qualities that are your core values, and reflect on what you already express, and also on what you would like to develop. How can you demonstrate these values daily in your life?

When you do, you will be in touch with your authentic, passionate being.

Affirmation: *I joyfully demonstrate my core values daily, creating a life of meaningful passion and authenticity.*

Morning - Today I intend to experience:

    1.

    2.

    3.

    4.

    5.

Evening – Tonight I express gratitude for whatever made me happy today:

    1.

    2.

    3.

    4.

    5.

Daily Success Tip:
Be Passionate

It will take too long and will be too difficult to learn how to succeed. (True or False?)

You already have the kernel of success within you. That kernel is "passion." If you find your passion, nothing can stop you to become the best you can be.

Make sure you find ways to tap into your passion. Do your goals inspire you? Are they aligned with your values? Do you have a sense of Purpose?

When you are in touch with your highest values and act in alignment with them, you have a springboard to your success, satisfaction, and being of greatest service to other people. Your passion will attract to you the situations you need for effortless success.

Affirmation: *I am passionate about my goals. They are meaningful to me, and my passion moves me forward effortlessly!*

Morning - Today I intend to experience:

    1.

    2.

    3.

    4.

    5.

Evening – Tonight I express gratitude for whatever made me happy today:

    1.

    2.

    3.

    4.

    5.

Day 11

Daily Success Tip:
Take Responsibility

Someone/something else is responsible for your life not working! (True or False?)

We hear that it is always the ex-spouse, the kids, the boss, our parents, the weather or the economy that has created havoc in our lives. The truth is that you are totally responsible for your success.

Your success is fully in your hands – always! Take a look at old mental programs that take away your power and motivation to reach your potential, and replace them with inner tapes that benefit you.

What do you think you "need" from someone else or something else that you can supply for yourself in some way? How can you begin fulfilling that need yourself?

What would your life look like if you took full responsibility?

Affirmation: *I am fully responsible for my life working, and for the success and well-being I choose.*

Morning - Today I intend to experience:
    1.
    2.
    3.
    4.
    5.

Evening – Tonight I express gratitude for whatever made me happy today:
    1.
    2.
    3.
    4.
    5.

Day 12

Daily Success Tip:
Create a Treasure Map

Of course, we know that New Years Resolutions do not work unless some additional factors come into play. Keeping continual focus on your goals is important.

Let's look at one way to keep them at least in our line of vision. One fun way is to create a **Treasure Map** – a simple but extremely powerful tool. Because many of us are visual learners, pictures of our goals make a deep and indelible imprint on our subconscious. Also, the process of looking for, finding, cutting out, and pasting the pictures gives us kinesthetic (muscular movement) involvement in the process, another key way to learn. Our goals become familiar to us, and thus, more realistic – more attainable. And, it's just plain fun!

The process:
1. Choose your goals.
2. Purchase a poster board.
3. Collect magazines.
4. Cut out pictures and words that represent your goals.
5. Paste them around the poster board in a colorful and pleasing way.

Finally, put your finished product somewhere that you can see it daily – or several times a day. Just glancing at the poster is enough. It works!

Affirmation: *I treasure my goals, and keep them in focus!*

Morning - Today I intend to experience:
  1.
  2.
  3.
  4.
  5.

Evening – Tonight I express gratitude for whatever made me happy today:
  1.
  2.
  3.
  4.
  5.

Day 13

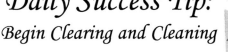

Daily Success Tip:
Begin Clearing and Cleaning

Simplifying and **clearing** clutter helps to **de-stress**. Cleaning up your physical universe is vital to mastery and forward movement. If things are not moving in your life, look around and see what needs to be cleared out!

Everything we own takes up mental space. Some part of our brain monitors every personal item at all times. What do you want on your mind? Can you locate everything in your household and office in ten seconds?

♦ **Action:**
> *Begin organizing, minimizing, categorizing and filing everything that is yours in this universe. Be ruthless about getting rid of "stuff."*

Clearing is necessary to make room for the "new" - new goals, situations, or dreams you choose for your life. Physical clarity leads to mental clarity.

And, think of others who would treasure some of the things you might consider trash, or just don't use anymore. Bless it, and let it go!

Affirmation: *I simplify and clear things in my physical environment, making room for new – new ideas, goals, and dreams!*

Morning - Today I intend to experience:

    1.

    2.

    3.

    4.

    5.

Evening – Tonight I express gratitude for whatever made me happy today:

    1.

    2.

    3.

    4.

    5.

Day 14

Daily Success Tip:
Take Action and Let Go

Your Winning Combination:

"If it is to be, it's up to me!" When you hear that adage, you probably want to roll up your sleeves and start working! Then, you hear, **"Let go and let God."** Oops, now it's time to take your hands off and sit back.

Successful people incorporate **BOTH** points of view into their lives. First, we must set our long range goals – describe what we want. Then – "let go and let God."

Next, we pay attention to the details of life as they appear – "if it is to be . . .." - all the time knowing, believing and expecting our goals to unfold easily and effortlessly. Watch closely to what you "attract" to you for hints that your goals are approaching!

Affirmation: *I know when to take action, and when to let go. That perfect rhythm attracts my success.*

56

Morning - Today I intend to experience:

1.
2.
3.
4.
5.

Evening – Tonight I express gratitude for whatever made me happy today:

1.
2.
3.
4.
5.

Day 15

Daily Success Tip:
Maintain Balance

Balance occurs when we nurture ourselves.   Ask yourself:

"How can I nurture myself every day?
- Do I want to meditate every morning?
- Will I honor my health with exercise and sensible nutrition?
- Will I invest in my well-being by spending my first waking moments listing on paper how I choose to "BE" that day?
- Will I ask others to assist?
- What is NOT necessary for my health, well-being and enjoyment of today – what can I eliminate from my to-do list?

Taking care of yourself FIRST is not selfish!   It is necessary, so that you will have enough to give. When you are filled – or fulfilled, it automatically spills over to others in a natural way.

Affirmation: *I choose to nurture myself today with healthy thoughts and actions. A sense of well-being and balance leads to my success.*

Morning - Today I intend to experience:
  1.
  2.
  3.
  4.
  5.

Evening – Tonight I express gratitude for whatever made me happy today:
  1.
  2.
  3.
  4.
  5.

Powerful Questions for Part II

These questions will help deepen your learning and experiences with the "Create Your Day With Intention" process.

Read over your Intentions for Part II.

1. What do you notice?

_____

_____

_____

_____

_____

2. Are you beginning to experience your days differently? If so, how?

_____

_____

_____

_____

_____

_____

_____

_____

_____

_____

_____

_____

_____

_____

Reflect on actions and decisions made while participating in Part II.

3. How can you benefit from learning to "let go" in your life?

_____

_____

_____

_____

_____

_____

_____

4. Can "letting go" and "cleaning and clearing" contribute to your sense of balance? How?

_____

_____

_____

_____

_____

_____

_____

5. Ask yourself, "What am I resisting?"

_____

_____

_____

_____

_____

_____

6. Will you let that resistance go?

_____
_____
_____
_____
_____
_____
_____
_____

7. How will you take exquisite care of your self?

_____
_____
_____
_____
_____
_____
_____
_____
_____
_____
_____
_____
_____
_____

Part III

Reflect

~Reflect~

After laying a strong foundation for your new life design, in **Part III** reflect on ways to enhance your natural ability to grow. Notice your inner and outer environment, and become aware of how you can nurture that genius within to move you forward toward your life's potential.

Day 16

Daily Success Tip:
Become a Success Magnet!

Are your dreams, goals, and wishes not manifesting fast enough? Do you seem to have roadblocks of frustration? Most of us who have had some coaching know how to set goals, use positive language and make affirmations. However, it seems easy to say, but sooooo easy to get distracted!

Our primary obstacle in setting and getting any goal is that we focus on the LACK of what we have at present. An example is this: I want to make more money, or have more fun in my life. What I am THINKING about is NOT having it at present. So, I am actually focused on lack of it.

Where should our focus be? **Experiencing an abundant life NOW**, so we can draw more to ourselves in the future. Begin enjoying and appreciating what you have, what you can do, and where you are right now. If "fun" is your goal, notice the moments, even nanoseconds, of fun you are experiencing at present, and appreciate them. If it is more money or a new job you want, notice the positive aspects of what you have now, and appreciate them. Feel good about them now. You will become a magnet for future success!

Affirmation: *I am now grateful for my abundance, and notice the fun, joy, and aliveness I experience today!*

66

Morning - Today I intend to experience:
   1.
   2.
   3.
   4.
   5.

Evening – Tonight I express gratitude for whatever made me happy today:
   1.
   2.
   3.
   4.
   5.

Day 17

Daily Success Tip:
Positives Attract Success

Thoughts and feelings act like magnets, attracting to us what we create in our lives. Have you noticed that people who are positive and optimistic attract positive outcomes? We may think they are positive BECAUSE good things have happened. However, their positive attitudes come FIRST.

How can you change or re-pattern our negative thoughts, feelings and expectations? One suggestion is that you create a **"Notebook of Positives,"** and list everything that is positive or beneficial to you about your work, your life, your family, a situation, etc., using one page for each topic. Make each list as extensive as you can. Then, to create the new patterns, allow yourself to focus on these benefits. Read these positive pages daily.

What we are really talking about is replacing old thoughts and feelings with new ones. Two thoughts cannot exist in the same place at the same time. It is to our benefit to choose the thought that supports our well-being, and helps us to "feel good." It takes practice, because it is soooo easy to slip into negative thoughts. They are more familiar, like a pair of old shoes. Like shoes, pick thoughts that support where you want to go – that new, high stepping, well-tread YOU!

Affirmation: *Today I invest my mind in positive thoughts and feelings, knowing that the return on my investment is success!*

68

Morning - Today I intend to experience:

    1.

    2.

    3.

    4.

    5.

Evening – Tonight I express gratitude for whatever made me happy today:

    1.

    2.

    3.

    4.

    5.

Day 18

Daily Success Tip:
Embrace Change

If you have been taught to "use your mind" to succeed in your career or personal life, then think again. Your mind-set, or beliefs, may be keeping you stuck in age-old, outworn, self-defeating patterns, like Sleeping Beauty under a spell. Most people today are eager to learn new tactics for a better career, or a better love life. But these fresh ideas fly out the window when faced with obstacles. We find ourselves reacting the same old ways we always have because our patterns run too deep.

You can break the enchantment by choosing new beliefs. Your new beliefs will support new behaviors and motivate you to the top. How does this work?

The purpose of the brain is to help you survive. Your old thought patterns and behavioral habits feel safe and comfortable, like a well-worn shoe. *Change* is fearful. Therefore, anything new is met with great resistance, and may not feel as safe.

Congratulate your mind when fear stalks you, because it is doing its job as a survival mechanism! Then, gently begin introducing your new thoughts. Choose a new belief or positive thought that supports your new goals and dreams.

> **Affirmation:** *I choose new beliefs and embrace the positive change that will unfold as I move forward in my life.*

Morning - Today I intend to experience:
1.
2.
3.
4.
5.

Evening – Tonight I express gratitude for whatever made me happy today:
1.
2.
3.
4.
5.

Day 19

Daily Success Tip:
Self-Acknowledgement

Who do you look to for acknowledgment? If you look for other people's acknowledgment, then you are not in control of your life! They are!

When you begin to spend time acknowledging yourself, then you can take your own steps toward balance and self-care. Who knows what we like or need or want better than ourselves?

Take stock. How good are you to yourself? Doing what is fulfilling to yourself FIRST leaves you brimming with goodness to share with others. If you try to acknowledge others first, you come from a position of neediness. So, fulfilling YOUR needs first is the name of the game.

So, the question is: How do you acknowledge yourself? How do you acknowledge and nurture your Mind, your Body and your Soul? How can you give yourself a mental "pat on the back" for your wins and accomplishments, or reward yourself in more tangible ways?

Affirmation: *I choose to acknowledge myself in Mind, Body and Soul by pursuing activities that are rewarding and fulfilling. I am in control of acknowledging me.*

Morning - Today I intend to experience:

    1.

    2.

    3.

    4.

    5.

Evening – Tonight I express gratitude for whatever made me happy today:

    1.

    2.

    3.

    4.

    5.

Day 20

Daily Success Tip:
Supportive Friends

Hang onto old acquaintances and friends – no matter what! (True or False?)

Have you noticed that people who are not working toward achieving their potential tend to group together? They are providing negative role models for each other by complaining and playing the "ain't it awful" games. The more you hear it, the deeper your conviction is that the negatives are true.

Conversely, if you begin to focus on and gravitate toward people who are winners, you will have positive role models for yourself. Often it is hard to let go of old-time associations, but the benefits are obvious. What would your friends look like and who would they be if they supported you to be your best?

What new choices will you make about friends?

Affirmation: *I choose friends who are positive, who inspire me, and who support my growth and success.*

Morning - Today I intend to experience:

    1.

    2.

    3.

    4.

    5.

Evening – Tonight I express gratitude for whatever made me happy today:

    1.

    2.

    3.

    4.

    5.

Day 21

Daily Success Tip:
Creative Thoughts

Worrying long enough will lead to a solution. (True or False?)

Worry is negative goal setting. The more you dwell on a negative idea or fear, the stronger it will become. Actually, it is when you mentally release and let go of a problem that your mind is free to be creative about possible solutions. Worry is an obstacle to finding solutions.

Catch yourself when you are worrying today. With what ideas can you replace those unproductive thoughts? What thoughts would actually benefit you? What could you say to yourself that would be supportive, motivating, heartfelt and loving? How can you unleash your creativity?

Affirmation: *I nurture thoughts that benefit me, that acknowledge me and motivate me toward my highest good and goals.*

Morning - Today I intend to experience:

    1.

    2.

    3.

    4.

    5.

Evening – Tonight I express gratitude for whatever made me happy today:

    1.

    2.

    3.

    4.

    5.

Day 22

Daily Success Tip:
Supportive Relationships

Relationships are a wonderful way to maintain balance in your life. People can be supportive in your personal or professional life, or both!

Using a car analogy, who in your life keeps your engine purring? Ask yourself who provides the following types of support:

- Comfort
- Clarification (and information)
- Confrontation
- Acknowledgment
- Energy givers.

Engine Diagnosis!
Now that we have your car up on the rack, let's look at these support categories. Ask yourself:
1. Which of the above categories have good support?
2. Which are lacking in support?
3. Do I rely on one or two people for support in many different categories?

Do your relationships need a tune-up? What actions will you take on insights from the above questions?

> **Affirmation:** *I am open to creating and accepting supportive relationships in my life today, and am grateful for their part in my success.*

Morning - Today I intend to experience:
     1.
     2.
     3.
     4.
     5.

Evening – Tonight I express gratitude for whatever made me happy today:
     1.
     2.
     3.
     4.
     5.

Powerful Questions for Part III

These questions will help deepen your learning and experiences with the "Create Your Day With Intention" process.

Read over your Intentions for Part III.

 1. What do you notice?

   _____
   _____
   _____
   _____
   _____

 2. Are you beginning to experience your days differently? If so, how?

   _____
   _____
   _____
   _____
   _____
   _____
   _____
   _____
   _____
   _____
   _____
   _____

_____

_____

Look over your notes from the "Reflect" section of Daily Intentions.

   3. Ask yourself, "Where do I limit myself?"

_____

_____

_____

_____

_____

_____

_____

_____

_____

   4. Ask, "What am I unwilling to risk?"

_____

_____

_____

_____

_____

_____

_____

_____

_____

5. Ask, "If I offered my best, what would I do right now, and who would I be?"

_____
_____
_____
_____
_____
_____
_____
_____
_____
_____
_____
_____
_____
_____
_____
_____

Part IV

Revitalize

~Revitalize~

In **Part IV** discover ways to maintain your momentum toward growth, keeping your natural genius by your side as your most treasured companion. Notice how you have become more "intentional" in your actions and your state of being daily. Notice the actions, thoughts and feelings that support your forward movement to becoming the brilliant architect of your new life design. Acknowledge ways in which you have begun to easily attract the results you desire, because you have become more attractive to yourself.

Day 23

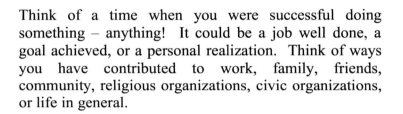

Daily Success Tip:
Draw From Strengths

Think of a time when you were successful doing something – anything! It could be a job well done, a goal achieved, or a personal realization. Think of ways you have contributed to work, family, friends, community, religious organizations, civic organizations, or life in general.

List what **strengths** you exhibited during these endeavors? Note your top strengths. Do you see any patterns among them? These are the qualities you offer to life, and to the achievement of your goals.

How can you use your strengths in current goals? How can focusing on your strengths increase your positive belief in yourself, and the esteem you bring to your endeavors? Acknowledging your qualities helps you to know you have a deep and abundant well of strengths from which to draw. Drink deeply!

Affirmation: *I acknowledge and draw from my strengths, drink deeply from them, and joyously offer them to the world.*

Morning - Today I intend to experience:

    1.

    2.

    3.

    4.

    5.

Evening – Tonight I express gratitude for whatever made me happy today:

    1.

    2.

    3.

    4.

    5.

Daily Success Tip:
Move Past Trauma and Change

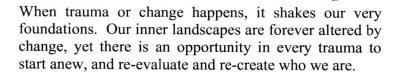

When trauma or change happens, it shakes our very foundations. Our inner landscapes are forever altered by change, yet there is an opportunity in every trauma to start anew, and re-evaluate and re-create who we are.

If trauma has happened to someone else close to us, we ask, "What can I do to help?" Being able to take action is healing, yet there may be little we can do. But, I invite you to look deeper – look within. What we all CAN do is re-visit our Life Purpose, if we know it, or re-affirm our core values. When our ground has shifted, we have the opportunity to make more meaningful priorities and begin to live them daily. We can affirm our resolve to express our values more authentically, as if it were our own last day and finest hour.

The world and our society could ask for nothing more HELPFUL and meaningful than this. Let trauma be a catalyst for living a more purposeful life.

> **Affirmation:** *I contribute to life in a significant way by staying in touch with and living my values and my Life Purpose.*

Morning - Today I intend to experience:

    1.

    2.

    3.

    4.

    5.

Evening – Tonight I express gratitude for whatever made me happy today:

    1.

    2.

    3.

    4.

    5.

Daily Success Tip:
Plant Seeds for Your Future

Are flowers blooming from all the seeds you planted in the past? Look at what you have in your life today. Like it or not, you paved the way for today's conditions and situations from thoughts and actions from the past.

A coaching client reinforced the process of manifesting using the powerful tool of coaching. "Linda" reported that she recently had a job offer that is tailor-made for her résumé. It is the same description of the "perfect" job she envisioned during coaching. However, she completed coaching a year ago! Her message was this: please tell your clients that it sometimes takes time to fulfill their dreams and for the "Universe" to put events into motion to bring what you want. Coaching continues to work even after the final handshake! What fun!

Affirmation: *Today I plant seeds for an abundant, joyful and successful future. I notice even small hints that these seeds are growing and will soon blossom.*

Morning - Today I intend to experience:

    1.

    2.

    3.

    4.

    5.

Evening – Tonight I express gratitude for whatever made me happy today:

    1.

    2.

    3.

    4.

    5.

Day 26

Daily Success Tip:
Check Your Battery

Do you take your car in for preventive maintenance? Imagine that you are on the way to close a huge sale, and the tires were flat, the battery had run down, or you were out of gas. You couldn't make it to the meeting. How effective would you be in closing that sale?

What about preventive maintenance in your life? What do you do to keep your motor purring, get the best gas mileage, as well as prolong your productivity?

Your Battery – Your Energy

Make a list of what drains your energy? *Is it negative relationships, lack of time management, poor diet, procrastination, lack of exercise and fresh air, lack of leisure and balance, or a difficult financial situation?*

Pick your top energy "drainer." How can you un-plug this drainer? What steps are you willing to take today to keep your battery of energy strong and powerful? What will happen if you don't make those steps?

Pick your best energy "givers." *Is it taking time off, watching a sunset, reading a book, getting a massage, learning something new, calling a good friend, gardening, or listening to cool music?*

How can you use this knowledge to maintain your vibrant aliveness and health?

Affirmation: *I keep my focus on what gives me energy. Positive energy attracts success.*

92

Morning - Today I intend to experience:

    1.

    2.

    3.

    4.

    5.

Evening – Tonight I express gratitude for whatever made me happy today:

    1.

    2.

    3.

    4.

    5.

Day 27

Daily Success Tip:
Focus on Fun

Being successful is not always a straightforward line consisting of hard work. In addition to training and ability, being successful is a matter of having:

1. Passion for what you do
2. Consistency, and
3. Focus.

How can you maintain your passion, consistency and focus? By weaving fun and leisure-time into every week – preferably every day! Imagine the difficulty you might have if you only worked! You get burned out, worn out, and tired. How effective can you be then?

So, fun and leisure are essential for your well-being and success, because after your enjoyable break, your passion and focus are restored. You are more willing to be consistent. You are on track! Also, you give room for creative ideas and new approaches to bubble-up when you take a break.

TAKE ACTION: Design your Ideal Week to include fun, play, leisure, and nurturing. It is a key to success! What better time to start than now?

> **Affirmation:** *I incorporate fun and leisure into my life today, knowing that they nurture, support and are essential to my success and well-being.*

Morning - Today I intend to experience:

    1.

    2.

    3.

    4.

    5.

Evening – Tonight I express gratitude for whatever made me happy today:

    1.

    2.

    3.

    4.

    5.

Day 28

Daily Success Tip:
Your Cheerleader

If you think great thoughts about yourself, you are conceited! (True or False?)

The truth is that you benefit from being your own best cheerleader. Conceit is just a cover-up for low self-esteem, and it sounds like bragging.

Telling ourselves – "You can do it!" and "Go for it" are indications of positive self-esteem.

These thoughts sound like optimism, and are the mark of true winners. Positive thoughts are "attractive."

Do you need to re-write your inner script? Incorporate new beliefs that help you demonstrate the esteem that attracts to you the success and well-being you want.

Affirmation: *I honor myself by being my own best cheerleader. I exhibit high self-esteem and attract my success.*

Morning - Today I intend to experience:

    1.

    2.

    3.

    4.

    5.

Evening – Tonight I express gratitude for whatever made me happy today:

    1.

    2.

    3.

    4.

    5.

Day 29

Daily Success Tip:
Giving

Although Goals and Clarity are topics that warm a coach's heart, there are other practices to attract success.

One is the concept of "Giving." Most of us focus on the receiving end of the flow cycle as we choose goals. However, sometimes we must "prime the pump." We step into that flow by participating in the movement of energy. For example, if you want to be a part of the energy flow of more money, first GIVE money away. Tradition provides us with the guideline of giving away 10% of our income to participate in that flow.

Do you want more referrals in your business? Then, spend a percentage of your time looking for referrals for other people. Do you want others to share their wisdom with you? Be willing to share your wisdom. Do you want to be invited to others' homes for dinner? Well, you get the picture!

The interesting thing about this flow of energy is that you do not have to give and get from the same place. You may give to someone behind "Door Number One," but receive from "Door Number Three." Somehow the Universal All knows that the flow has been acknowledged. When you give, a vacuum is created, and there is room for more to flow back to you.

Affirmation: *I step into the flow of abundant life by giving – especially to the sources of my inspiration.*

Morning - Today I intend to experience:
     1.
     2.
     3.
     4.
     5.

Evening – Tonight I express gratitude for whatever made me happy today:
     1.
     2.
     3.
     4.
     5.

Day 30

Daily Success Tip:
Powerful Partnerships

It is a sign of failure, an admission of weakness, or embarrassing to look for help with success. (True or False?)

There is no greater way to attain success than having a one-on-one relationship with a positive, successful mentor or coach. A coach mirrors back to you your strengths and helps you get in touch with your passion.

Books, tapes and seminars are great for new ideas, but it takes an on-going, supportive role model to help you break old habits, stay in focus, and use all the good ideas you have gathered in your lifetime for your success.

It is considered a strength to know when and where to find guidance along your journey. Even with your knowledge and wisdom, a coach or mentor can help you maximize your gifts, and point out areas for development. Partnering with someone for accountability is a savvy, admirable step!

Affirmation: *I choose partners for support, focus and accountability on my journey to success. Supportive partnerships are powerful!*

Morning - Today I intend to experience:

    1.

    2.

    3.

    4.

    5.

Evening – Tonight I express gratitude for whatever made me happy today:

    1.

    2.

    3.

    4.

    5.

Powerful Questions for Part IV

These questions will help deepen your learning and experiences with the "Create Your Day With Intention" process.

Read over your Intentions for Part IV.

    1. What do you notice?

_____
_____
_____
_____
_____

    2. Are you beginning to experience your days differently? If so, how?

_____
_____
_____
_____
_____
_____
_____
_____
_____
_____
_____
_____
_____
_____

Reflect on your notes and actions from Part IV and ask yourself these questions:

3. What excites me about my life in the present?

_____

_____

_____

_____

_____

_____

_____

_____

_____

4. What are my major commitments?

_____

_____

_____

_____

_____

_____

_____

_____

_____

5. Am I becoming intentional about my day?

_____

_____

_____

_____

6. Am I expressing gratitude to others and myself? If so, what difference is that making?

_____
_____
_____
_____
_____
_____
_____
_____
_____

7. How will I use the concepts in this book to move forward more powerfully in my life?

_____
_____
_____
_____
_____
_____
_____
_____
_____

Celebrate!

Come celebrate with us!

Completion also heralds a new beginning. By allowing new thoughts and behaviors for 30 days, you have created new patterns of setting intentions, expressing gratitude, and becoming "attractive" to what you want. You have re-created yourself in a positive, life-affirming way. Spirit thanks you!

~ Ask Yourself ~

Self- Assessment

After you have completed the 30-day program, ask yourself the following questions to rate your mastery over the items. Each mastery point corresponds to a Daily Tip. Rate the degree to which you have mastered each point, with 1 being a low rating, and 10 being a high rating. Re-read the Daily Tips that correspond to areas that need improvement, and design actions to strengthen those areas.

1. I set intentions for my day. (1 2 3 4 5 6 7 8 9 10)

2. I end my day expressing gratitude for things that made me happy.
    (1 2 3 4 5 6 7 8 9 10)

3. I have developed a Future Vision for my life. (1 2 3 4 5 6 7 8 9 10)

4. I have clear goals, and enjoy watching them unfold.
    (1 2 3 4 5 6 7 8 9 10)

5. My goals and results are set for all areas of my life for balance.
    (1 2 3 4 5 6 7 8 9 10)

6. I am willing to move toward my goals by recognizing and continually letting go of resistance. (1 2 3 4 5 6 7 8 9 10)

7. I have identified my first small step toward my goals, and expect the other steps to unfold effortlessly.   (1 2 3 4 5 6 7 8 9 10)

8. I participate in co-creating my life by designing dreams and allowing myself to stretch. (1 2 3 4 5 6 7 8 9 10)

9. I know my core values and joyfully demonstrate them in my life and work daily. (1 2 3 4 5 6 7 8 9 10)

10. My goals are meaningful to me, and my passion motivates me to move forward toward my goals. (1 2 3 4 5 6 7 8 9 10)

11. I am fully responsible for my life working and for the success and well-being I choose. (1 2 3 4 5 6 7 8 9 10)

12. I treasure my goals and keep them in focus with supportive processes like "Treasure Mapping." (1 2 3 4 5 6 7 8 9 10)

13. I simplify and clear things in my physical environment, making room for new ideas, goals and dreams! (1 2 3 4 5 6 7 8 9 10)

14. I know when to take action, and when to let go. (1 2 3 4 5 6 7 8 9 10)

15. I nurture myself daily, knowing that balance leads to my success. (1 2 3 4 5 6 7 8 9 10)

16. I focus on what I HAVE rather than what I LACK to manifest my desires. (1 2 3 4 5 6 7 8 9 10)

17. When I feel challenged by another person or by situations, I use my "Notebook of Positives" to shift my focus and allow my good to unfold. (1 2 3 4 5 6 7 8 9 10)

18. I choose new beliefs and embrace the positive change that will unfold as I move forward in my life. (1 2 3 4 5 6 7 8 9 10)

19. I acknowledge myself in Mind, Body and Soul by pursuing activities that are rewarding and fulfilling. (1 2 3 4 5 6 7 8 9 10)

20. I choose friends who are positive, who inspire me, and who support my growth and success. (1 2 3 4 5 6 7 8 9 10)

21. I nurture thoughts that benefit me, that acknowledge me and motivate me toward my highest good and goals. (1 2 3 4 5 6 7 8 9 10)

22. I have supportive relationships in my life. (1 2 3 4 5 6 7 8 9 10)

23. I know and acknowledge my strengths, and use them to achieve my goals. (1 2 3 4 5 6 7 8 9 10)

24. When I experience trauma or great change in my life, I see an opportunity to acknowledge my values, to re-create my life and to inspire others. (1 2 3 4 5 6 7 8 9 10)

25. Daily I plant seeds for my personal and professional well-being, then watch patiently for clues that they are sprouting and ready to blossom. (1 2 3 4 5 6 7 8 9 10)

26. I know that positive energy attracts success, and I manage my energy carefully. (1 2 3 4 5 6 7 8 9 10)

27. I allow for fun daily, knowing that balance in life is an essential ingredient to attract success. (1 2 3 4 5 6 7 8 9 10)

28. I feel confident and exhibit high self-esteem. (1 2 3 4 5 6 7 8 9 10)

29. Giving to others is easy for me, and my generosity stimulates the flow of abundance. (1 2 3 4 5 6 7 8 9 10)

30. I choose supportive partners for focus and accountability to help me in life's journey. (1 2 3 4 5 6 7 8 9 10)

Shifting to the Next Level After the First 30 Days

Attracting What You Want:

Have you ever had something "fall in your lap" when you least expected it – good fortune smiled on you just after you let go of wanting it? This is "Attracting What You Want" in a nutshell. Instead of working your fingers to the bone to achieve a goal, wouldn't you like to have it show up in your life more easily, without forceful effort?

The secret is this: attraction is about "inner" work first. Rather than trying to make something happen, which brings up resistance and effort, you can shift to attracting goals by <u>being</u> in a state of enjoyment. Notice that the "Be-ing" comes first.

Now, that does not mean you can sit around and contemplate your navel all day, eat grapes and sit by the pool. You can, however, shift your focus, so that struggle and hard work are eliminated.

Attraction does include the word "action." There are still action steps to be taken, but achieving through attraction means that the actions to be taken are more harmonious, thoughtful, efficient, and hopefully fun! Why use a sledgehammer when the light-feather touch will suffice?

By applying your "inner work" first, you are more still, quiet, and able to feel or hear those inner nudges from your Higher Self, your intuition, or the Universal All. The "inner work" helps you to remove obstacles to the Source of All Knowledge, so you are shown the path to your desires more clearly.

What is this "inner work?" Spending time each day contemplating the "Daily Tips" is your jump-start. Setting your intentions based on who you choose to be that day, and also expressing gratitude comprise "inner work." You have already begun this journey.

Most of us would rather roll our sleeves up and start moving ahead, doing, doing, doing, but laying a firm foundation with contemplative time is the key to shifting to a higher level of personal achievement.

Delving Deeper:

Now that you have experienced the concepts in the "Daily Tips," these next steps are suggested.

Steps for "After the First 30 Days"

1. Choose a "Tip" that speaks to you. Or, flip through the book, and see where your gaze lands.
2. Spend time with the concepts in the "Tip" you chose, until you make it your own and have integrated it into your life.
3. Use the Visualization Process to deepen your learning. (*see next page*)
4. Continue the practice of setting intentions and expressing daily gratitude.
5. Choose another "Tip" and repeat the process above.

Visualization
To Create a Powerful Intention

Note: Read over the visualization process until you are familiar with it. You may also record this on tape, allowing for pauses, and listen to it as it guides you through the process. If done in a group, one person can read the script for the others.

Choose an area of change or refinement for yourself. State what you want or choose in positive terms, as if you are already that person you choose to be. You may use your own affirmation, or positive statement, or take one from a "Tips" page in the book. Write your statement on a piece of paper.

Gently close your eyes, and begin to take deep breaths. Settle into your seated or prone position, and allow relaxation to envelope you. Starting at your feet, say, "Toes and feet, relax." Move your attention up your body, and say, "Legs, relax." Then, "Abdomen and stomach, relax." Then, "Heart area and neck, relax." Then, "Face relax." Spend a few moments relaxing the face muscles, the mouth, the cheeks, the forehead, and the tongue. The face and head can bring relaxation to the rest of the body. Sweep your inner gaze over your whole body, and mentally request that any tight spots now relax and let go.

Enjoy the smooth, calm relaxing moment.

When you are ready, imagine that a bright, white light is entering the top of your head, and flowing down into your heart area. Let this bright light warm your heart

113

and allow the warmth to accumulate, build and grow larger and larger.

Allow your inner self to begin reflecting on the new aspect of yourself to develop, as stated in the affirmation you chose. Hold the piece of paper with your affirmation/desire on it next to your heart. Take key words from your affirmation, and imagine they are floating within the bright light in your heart. Then, in your mind's eye, see this light with your key words moving forward, out of your body, and into the universe, and beyond. Your bright light and desires connect with a distant star, which intensifies the essence of your thoughts and your key words.

Imagine that, once intensified, the light and thoughts loop back and find their way back into the crown of your head. Welcome the lightness and intensity of your desire, and watch as it moves down into your heart center once again, to support and embellish your inner creation. See, feel or know that there is a great loop of light connecting your desires to the Source, and the Source is also connected to you.

Know that you now are aided by the energy of the stars and higher forces to become the person you choose to be, with the new aspects of yourself that you have chosen.

Breathe deeply, and say, "Welcome" to the new you. Know that your changes have occurred on the cellular level, and have blended with higher powers.

Smile fully and express gratitude for this creation. Take deep breaths, enjoy the warmth of your heart, smile again, and allow yourself to open your eyes when you feel ready.

Books & Resources

Belf, Teri-E. Coaching with Spirit

Belf, Teri-E. and Ward, Charlotte. Simply Live it Up

Dwoskin, Hale. The Sedona Method

Escudé, Vicki. Getting Everything You Want and Going for more! Coaching for Mastery

Grabhorn, Lynn. Excuse Me, Your Life is Waiting

Hawkins, David R. Power vs. Force

Hicks, Esther and Jerry, Ask and It Is Given

King, Joan. Cellular Wisdom

Tolle, Eckhart. The Power of Now

Ward, Charlotte and Belf, Teri-E. Auto Suggestions

Organization and Time Management: Time/Design
www.timedesign.com

Professional Coaching Resources:
Executive Leadership Coaching, LLC,
www.excellentcoach.com, vicki@excellentcoach.com

Success Unlimited Network®, LLC, (SUN)
www.successunlimitednet.com

Strategic Executive Coaching Alliance (SECA)
www.seca-1.com

International Coach Federation (ICF),
www.coachfederation.org

About the Author

Vicki H. Escudé, M.A., MCC is a Master Certified Coach, and is CEO of Executive Leadership Coaching, LLC. She coaches individuals, and trains and certifies coaches worldwide, and has been recognized as a successful coach in national publications. She is certified by Success Unlimited Network®, LLC, an internationally recognized and acclaimed coaching program designed to empower people to get results in their lives. She also has the highest-level certification awarded by the International Coach Federation and was elected to the Board of Directors of the ICF for 2005 – 2007. Escudé is a senior associate of SECA, a corporate coaching and training organization.

Escudé is passionate about helping people find their Life Purpose, so they may create and live a life of meaning and fulfillment.

Escudé received a BA degree from Vanderbilt University, and an MA degree from the University of West Florida in psychology and counseling. She lives in Savannah, Georgia, and Avon, Colorado.

Cover design by Clark Creative